THE VIKINGS

WRITTEN AND ILLUSTRATED BY

JOHN FARRELLY

THE O'BRIEN PRESS
DUBLIN

Dedication

For Ellie – who invaded Ireland in her own way.

Acknowledgements

I'd like to thank OBP for the opportunity to do this book; my good buddy Garry for his endless enthusiasm and my family and friends for their encouragement (ie 'You couldn't write your way out of a paper bag, Farrelly!' 'Is that supposed to be a drawing of a Viking?' etc. etc.).

First published 2020 by The O'Brien Press Ltd,
12 Terenure Road East, Rathgar, Dublin 6, D06 HD27, Ireland.
Tel: +353 1 4923333; Fax: +353 1 4922777
E-mail: books@obrien.ie
Website: www.obrien.ie
The O'Brien Press is a member of Publishing Ireland.

ISBN: 978-1-78849-103-7

Copyright for text and illustrations © John Farrelly
Design: Brendan O'Reilly
Copyright for typesetting, layout, editing, design
© The O'Brien Press Ltd

1 3 5 7 6 4 2
20 22 24 23 21

Printed and bound by Norhaven Paperback A/S, Denmark.
The paper in this book is produced using
pulp from managed forests

Published in

DUBLIN
UNESCO
City of Literature

CONTENTS

SO WHO WERE THESE VIKINGS, THEN?

Well, for a start *viking* was something they did, not something they were. They called themselves *Norraener Menn* or Norse Men, and the first wave of Vikings came from Norway. The Irish sometimes called them *Lochlannaigh*, 'men from the land of lakes'. The monks whose monasteries they raided in the 9th century called them 'pagans' or 'heathens'. To go 'a-viking' meant to go off on a boat somewhere in search of gold and adventure, and the Vikings were very good at viking, so the name stuck. These warriors from the cold north earned a fearsome reputation for killing, looting and pillaging.

They were feared so much that one Irish monk wrote a poem being thankful for a wet and windy night as Vikings only ever came when the seas were calm.

Fierce is the wind tonight,
It tosses the sea's white mane;
I need not fear the violent
warriors from Norway
Crossing the Irish Sea.

If newspapers had been around back then, we may have seen headlines like these about them:

Ye Olden Times

AD 795

IRISH MONASTERY RAIDED BY VIKINGS

DOZENS KILLED

The surviving members of a sleepy island community of monks were left traumatised after a lightning raid by foreign savages earlier today.

Dozens of monks were murdered while others were beaten or taken prisoner at the monastic settlement on Rechru Island, just off the coast of

Rechru Island

WEATHER: Look at your window, dearie!

Past Times

A.D. 798   1 GROAT

PILLAGE IDIOTS!
VIKINGS AT IT AGAIN!

YESTERDAY'S NEWS

VIKING PLUNDER WONDER!
Connacht attacked

AD 807

Then again, the Vikings were no more savage than other people throughout history ...

WORLD 🌐 NEWS

AD1221

GENGHIS KHAN MURDERS 40 MILLION PEOPLE

"If anybody can, Genghis Khan," says aide.

THE MOON

AD1462

VLAD IMPALES 100,000

Competition to give Vlad a nickname on page 5!

Bad Lad Vlad Tad Mad

HOROSCOPES PAGE 9

Daily Olds

BINGO PAGE 12

AD1490

SPANISH INQUISITION - 1000s DEAD
Torquemada "very pleased".

And let's not forget, the Irish weren't exactly boy scouts themselves ...

VOTED THE 4th CENTURY'S BEST OLDSPAPER!

Irish Chronicle

AD399

BOY (16) SOLD INTO SLAVERY BY IRISH PIRATES

Story by
Muirchú Mór

"It's not like he's a saint or anything," pirate leader says, "but snakes seem to be afraid of him."

Irish snakes defiant:
"We're here to sssstay!"

hibernia ✠ today

AD588

DRUIDS SACRIFICE KING

"The crops failed so we gave him the old one, two, three," says spokesdruid.

"You just don't see it a lot any more," said one elderly man, "what with us supposed to be Christians and that. So when I heard it was happening, I got the wife and grandkids and we watched the whole lot while eating some bread, cheese and

mutton. Got good seats and everything, near the front. I know he's our king and all, but the crops failed so it's his fault. He is the land and the land is him, so he had to go."

The ritual, known as the "threefold-death" took

So if the Vikings were only as bad as everybody else, why do they live on in everybody's memory as marauding, murdering maniacs? Why did they appear from nowhere and attack monasteries in Britain and Ireland in a series of violent raids that were over faster than you could say Jormungand Mjolnir Svartalfheim Yggdrasil,* then disappear back over the horizon in their amazing ships? Why did they decide to come and live in Ireland after all the naughty things they'd done there? And were they really as savage, uncivilized and **DEADLY!** as we are led to believe? Let's find out ...

*YOU'LL DISCOVER WHAT ALL THESE THINGS ARE BY THE END OF THE BOOK, DON'T WORRY!

HOME IS WHERE THE HEARTH IS
EARLY SCANDINAVIA & IRELAND

This is what life was like for Irish people back in the good old 8th century:

They had roundhouses

druids and priests

slaves

filí – poets who told stories

kings, chieftains and nobles

freemen who worked the land

and warriors who fought for their chieftains and raided their neighbours for treasure and slaves.

And this is what life was like for Viking people back in the good old 8th century:

They had longhouses

kings, jarls and nobles

skald – poets who told stories

gothi and gythia

thralls (slaves)

freemen who worked the land

and warriors who fought for their jarl and raided their neighbours for treasure and thralls.

Not so very different, are they?

13

The Scandinavian summers were shorter and their winters longer than Irish ones and so crops were harder to grow. And though Scandinavia was huge, the land was hard and rocky and as the population grew, the Vikings fought each other for what good land was left.

There were no such problems in Ireland – it had plenty of decent farming land and huge forests filled with wild deer, pigs and hares, as well as rivers brimming with salmon and trout. The climate was mild, if a little wet at times (some things never change!) and there was plenty of rich grassland for cattle to graze on.

The Vikings weren't Christians, but Ireland was known as 'the land of saints and scholars' because it had loads of churches and monasteries. Famous Irish monasteries, like the one at Clonmacnoise, attracted people from all over Europe.

Although the Church was wealthy, the monks lived a simple life. One monk called Columba said he had 'bare rock for his bed, and a stone for a pillow'.

There were loads of rules to follow and the monks were severely punished if they broke any. It was no picnic being an Irish monk in the 8th century! But without the Irish monks, a lot of knowledge would have been lost and beautiful illuminated manuscripts like the Book of Kells – which you can go and see in Trinity College in Dublin – would never have existed.

Apart from books, the monasteries were also full of other things, like gold chalices, silver candlesticks and crosses encrusted with precious jewels, making them a very juicy target.

This is Brother 'Porky' Peadar. Even though he's a Christian, he's been known to 'bear false witness' sometimes. Which of his statements do you think are true? **Answers below.**

A) WE MONKS PRAY THREE TIMES A DAY.

B) WE BUILT TALL ROUND TOWERS SO WE COULD HIDE FROM RAIDERS.

C) IT TAKES 25 ANIMAL SKINS TO MAKE 100 SHEETS OF PARCHMENT FOR THE BOOKS WE WRITE.

D) WE'RE NOT ALLOWED TO EAT MEAT.

E) SOMETIMES WE USE GOLD FOR THE COVERS OF OUR BOOKS.

ANSWERS: Brother Peadar told only three lies, bless him. a) The monks prayed up to nine times a day! b) Probably false. Most of the round towers were built from the 11th century onwards and so came after the Vikings. c) True! d) False. Monks ate quite well, though they had to have fish on Fridays and fast on certain days. e) Yep! Raiders would steal the books not for the writing inside, but for the cover! Though sometimes they would use the calfskin pages as insoles for their shoes!

I JUST ROWED IN FROM NORWAY AND NOW MY ARMS ARE REALLY THOR

THE VIKING LONGSHIP

The Vikings were brilliant shipbuilders and they made different kinds of ships for different things. They are best known for the big, fast, seaworthy longships that they called *drakkar* (meaning dragons) but they also had other ships, including ones called *snekkar* (meaning snakes), which were smaller and lighter than drakkar.

The longship was the Ferrari of the seas at the time – it was the fastest boat in the world. Not only could some Viking ships sail upriver and be carried overland, they could also go forwards or backwards. These ships were designed to be rowed by the crew when the wind wasn't strong enough to power the sail.

A DEADLY! GUIDE TO ...
BUILDING A LONGSHIP

1) Cut down a tall oak tree and shape it with tools called **adzes** to make the bottom of the ship – the keel. Set this on top of a load of planks to keep it dry. Then join the bow (front) and stern (back) to the keel.

2) Cut *strakes* (planks) from trees and attach them together using iron rivets. Attach crossbeams and curved wooden ribs to the strakes using wooden pegs – **trenails** – to make the strakes stronger. Place a big block of wood with a slot cut in it at the bottom of the ship to hold the mast.

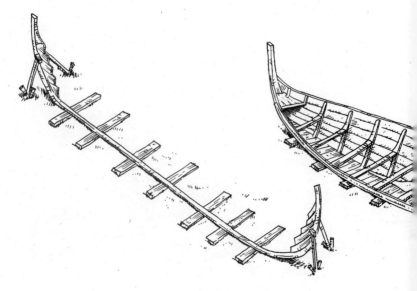

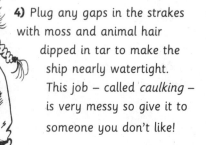

3) Drill holes for the oars into the sides and lay the deck. Add a fish-shaped block (called a **mast-fish**, funny enough!) to keep the mast upright, as well as some supports that are used for storing the mast, sail and oars when they're not being used. Attach a **steering oar** to the stern.

#©☠米!!!

4) Plug any gaps in the strakes with moss and animal hair dipped in tar to make the ship nearly watertight. This job – called *caulking* – is very messy so give it to someone you don't like!

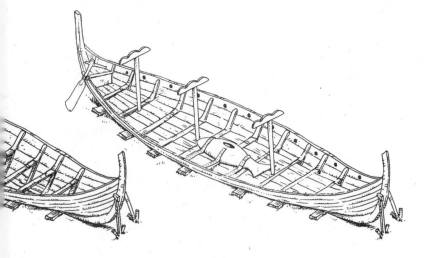

It took a long time and a lot of skill to build a ship. When it was finally ready, the chieftain or *jarl* would appoint a leader of the expedition who would then choose his crew, who were mostly young men and farmers *(karls)*.

They were just ordinary men who went raiding in between sowing their crops and taking in the harvest. While they were gone, the women would often take over running the farm.

Say hello to Snorri the Fib-Teller. Sometimes he's a wee bit economical with the truth. Which of his statements do you think are true? **Answers below.**

A) A VIKING LONGSHIP CAN TRAVEL 100 KM IN ONE DAY.

B) A VIKING SHIP IS AS LONG AS THE PITCH AT CROKE PARK.

C) IT TAKES 70 TREES TO BUILD A LONGSHIP.

D) IT TAKES THE WOOL OF 500 SHEEP TO MAKE THE SAIL FOR A LONGSHIP.

E) THE MAST ON A LONGSHIP IS 25 M TALL.

ANSWERS: Snorri is a right liar. **ALL** those statements are false. a) A Viking longship could travel 190 km in a single day. b) A typical longship was 30 m in length, so Croke Park is about 5 ships long and 3 ships wide. c) It took 91 oak, willow, pine and ash trees, to make one ship. d) It took the wool from 1,000 sheep to make the sail. That's a lot of naked sheep! e) The mast on a typical Viking ship was 16 m tall.

DEADLY! CRUISE COMPANY

Do you want to spend weeks on a cold, cramped, uncomfortable ship with sixty other men?

Do you want to share a *húdfat* (sleeping bag) with

someone who has had dried fish, pickled meat and sour milk for his dinner?

Do you want to spend most of your free time bailing out stinking bilge water?

THEN COME WITH US ON A NORSE LONGSHIP CRUISE!

THE LONGSHIP

Although the first longships that brought the Vikings to Ireland were built in Norway, a ship similar to the one on the next few pages was found sunk in a harbour in Denmark that was made from oak trees possibly felled in Glendalough, Co. Wicklow in the year 1042. This means that the Vikings must have built longships in Ireland after they settled there.

After all the food and water supplies were loaded, as well as shields and weapons, it was a pretty tight squeeze aboard the ship. As they couldn't very well light a fire to cook food aboard a wooden ship, the men brought dried meat and fish, as well as barrels of sour milk (YUCK!) and fresh water. Just in case they were close enough to shore to be able to light a fire and cook something hot, like a nice mutton stew, they also took a cauldron – a big cooking pot.

A WEEK OR MORE TO GET THERE ...

... A WEEK OR MORE TO GET BACK.

NORWAY

The voyage between Norway and Ireland took at least a week and sometimes much longer, so they had to bring enough supplies for the journey there and back.

Each man had a sea-chest to keep his stuff safe and he sat on this when the ship had to be rowed. **Can you tell what these belongings are just from their silhouettes?** Answers below.

1.

The helmsman kept the ship on course using the steering-oar.

2.

3.

4.

Even hardy sailors could get sea-sick sometimes!

ANSWERS: 1) Helmet. Whether it's made of leather or iron, never go anywhere without your helmet. 2) Knife. Vikings used these for whittling wood but could be useful in close combat! 3) Drinking horn. Made from cow or goat horn, this couldn't be put down when it was full so you had to drink the lot in one go. 4) Thor's hammer amulet. Sailors wore this for protection. (More lore about Thor you will adore late-or.)

24

Although the ship was nearly watertight, plenty of buckets and scoops were kept onboard to bail out bilge water when the sea got rough – which was often! If there weren't enough buckets, they used their helmets.

No he's not taking a selfie. Vikings may have used a 'sunstone' to navigate when it got cloudy. And the seas around Ireland were always cloudy! Other ways they navigated were by the stars and watching for birds that flew near land.

The Vikings carved ugly figureheads to scare away the evil gods of the sea and to terrify their enemies. Maybe they used your older brother or sister as a model! Sometimes these were dragon heads.

This made many people call the longboats 'dragon ships', which does sound pretty cool!

AAAAIIIEEE!!

So life onboard a longship wasn't exactly comfortable. Ever ridden a bicycle downhill on a rainy day with the ice-cold wind stinging your cheeks? (Whaddaya mean, 'No'? You really need to get out more!) Well, that's what it was like on the deck of a longship ... for days on end. If you got sick and died on the voyage, you simply got chucked overboard.

Whatever free time you had (if it was calm and after you'd taken your turn rowing or bailing), you could have a nap or play a board game called *Hnefatafl*. More on that later. When the voyage wasn't totally boring ... it could be utterly terrifying!

So why go?

FOR THE *BLING!* YAAAGGGH!!!

SPEAR ME THE GRUESOME DETAILS

FIRST RAIDS ON IRELAND

Apart from their own land becoming overcrowded, and having a liking for gold, why did the Vikings leave Scandinavia and suddenly start attacking monasteries on the coasts of England, Ireland and Scotland when they had been trading peacefully with those places for years?

Ireland was a beautiful fertile place (still is!), but back in Viking times it was a land of warring tribes. And despite everyone saying they were Christians, they often raided each other's lands, stealing cattle and capturing people to take as slaves. Saint Patrick was a Roman-British boy who had been kidnapped by *Irish* raiders.

Sometimes the warring tribes even raided the monasteries on the land of neighbouring tribes. Clonmacnoise monastery was raided at least 27 times by Irish raiders, but only 7 times by Vikings.

The first recorded Viking attack on an Irish monastery was on Rechru Island (either Rathlin Island on the north coast or Lambay Island near Dublin — the experts can't agree) in the year 795, right around the time that Emperor Charlemagne (Charles the Great) was expanding his empire throughout Europe. He was pretty aggressive about this, killing any 'heathens' who did not convert to Christianity.

As he moved northwards he targeted the Saxons and in one especially nasty encounter took 4,500 Saxons down to a river, baptised them and then cut all their heads off. Nice fella.

So what has this got to do with the Vikings? Well, Saxony, where the Saxons lived, was just a stone's throw away from Scandinavia which is where the Vikings lived.

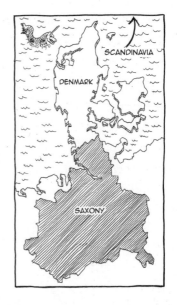

They would definitely have heard about this Charlemagne and his deeds. And so, some people think, the Vikings decided to strike first by attacking centres of Christian worship — the monasteries. The Vikings had no respect for Christian faith at that time; it was a strange religion to them, with nice, big, fat unguarded monasteries full of goodies and monks who couldn't fight. And because the Irish were fighting amongst themselves, nobody wanted to team up against the Vikings. It would be stupid of them *not* to raid these places.

Raiding was nothing new to Vikings — they'd been doing it round their own lands for a long time before they came to Ireland. It was just a natural part of life to them, like the way we pop down to the shops for a carton of milk. Raiding fitted in with the Viking values of honour, comradeship and ruthlessness. Mercy was seen as a weakness and Christianity as a weak religion.

And now it's time for the news ...

Yes, the Vikings even took monks as slaves. Before we judge them too harshly, remember that many 'civilized' Americans still owned slaves just over 150 years ago. Slavery was (and still is) common in many cultures – including Christian ones. As the Vikings saw it, they were no more cruel than the Christian armies who were slaughtering their way across Europe.

A DEADLY! GUIDE TO ...
PILLAGING A MONASTERY

1) Park the longships on the beach. Leave a few men to guard them, otherwise there's a chance someone will come along and burn them. Then there's no going home!

2) Run up the beach shouting and waving your axe about to frighten the monks.

3) Grab anything shiny – gold, jewels, silver – and burn what's left. Some say the Vikings believed the spirits of those who they killed would follow them home if they didn't destroy the lot.

4) Take some monks who look like they might make good thralls (slaves), but no old ones (anyone over age 25). You can kill any who look like they might give you trouble by a) drowning or b) an axe in the face. Don't worry, they won't have any weapons to hurt *you* with.

5) Head back to the ships pronto before anyone has time to raise the alarm.

6) Sail back to Norway with your nice new belongings.

When the Vikings returned home from the first raid with a ship full of booty and slaves, the king or jarl (chieftain) who paid for the expedition must have been delighted. Also, because of the swiftness of the attack and the fact they met no resistance, none of the Vikings were killed  or injured. It was like taking candy from a baby.

And so, they did what any good baby-candy thief would do – they came back again and again to different island monasteries.

Once, they attacked Skellig Michael off the south-west coast and captured the abbot called Étgal. They held the poor man prisoner and demanded a ransom for his safe return. When nobody paid up, they starved him to death.

This pattern of lightning raids on monasteries happened about once a year. Because it was not known exactly when or where they might attack, the Irish couldn't prepare an army. Though some Irish tribes did strike back when they got the chance.

All people could do was to keep a good look-out for the dragon ships that could appear at any moment, then raise the alarm when they did. The furthest distance the ships could be seen from land was about 30 km and it could've taken the Vikings about a couple of hours to sail that. So this meant people had very little time to grab their stuff and run for their lives when the Vikings landed!

Which belongings would *you* take?

1) Silver chalice

2) Silver crucifix

3) Gold book cover

4) Gold candlesticks

5) Reliquary (complete with saint's bones)

If you were smart, you'd grab stuff that's light enough to carry and some food and water then head inland where the Viking raiders won't follow.

It was bad enough waiting for Viking raiders to turn up and start looting and pillaging, but at least they kept to isolated islands and coasts so they could make a quick getaway.

For a while anyhow. After attacking Ireland for 40 years and getting better at it each time, the Vikings made their first inland – not on the coast – raid on the lands of the southern Uí Néill (in English, O'Neill) tribe in Co. Meath. Because the Uí Néills were not expecting this, the raid went rather well and the Vikings killed loads of people and took lots of captives. Ooh, those pesky Vikings had gone and done it this time!

By attacking a powerful Irish clan like the Uí Néills deep in their own territory, the Vikings were making it clear they weren't to be messed with. Part of their success was because their longships could sail just as well in shallow rivers as they did in the sea. And also because the Vikings were mad enough to carry the ships over land. Yes, really!

A DEADLY! GUIDE TO ...
CARRYING A VIKING WARSHIP OVER LAND

If the Vikings were sailing up a river and there was a stretch of land between them and the next river-bend, it was sometimes quicker just to lift the boat out of water and take it across land rather than sail around it. This was called *portage*. Here's how you would do it:

1) Pull the boat up onto the land and empty everything out of it – including the mast, sail, sea-chests* – everything except the oars.

2) Cut down some trees and slice 'em up into big logs with a round side and a flat side.

3) Grease the round sides of the logs with old lard or rotting fish guts. Mmm ... YUM!

4) Lay the logs out in a row in front of the ship with the flat side facing down and the round side facing up.

5) Push the oars through the oar-holes on both sides of the ship.

6) Push the longship over the greased logs, while runners grab the logs from the back of the ship and run forward to put them at the front again.

7) Repeat the process until the ship is across the stretch of land. Try to stay on course so as not to damage the ship or let it get out of control.

I TOLD YOU GUYS TO SLOW DOWN OR THIS WOULD HAPPEN!

Don't forget to go back for the mast, sail and sea-chests!

A NORSE PLACE TO LIVE

VIKING TOWNS

When the Vikings first turned up in Ireland and started killing, stealing and setting fire to things, at least they went back home. Now, around forty years later, it looked like they had taken quite a liking to Ireland and wanted to stay – PERMANENTLY! Would you like to have been neighbours with them?

But whether the Irish liked it or not, in 837 sixty ships full of Vikings arrived from Norway. This time they went even further inland – right up the River Liffey and the Boyne, plundering farms, churches and fortresses along the way. In 840, they spent the whole winter on Lough Neagh in the north — the first winter they spent away from home.

IRISH WINTERS ARE NEARLY AS GOOD AS NORWEGIAN SUMMERS!

The Vikings knew they would feel about as welcome as a fox in a hen-house after all their bad behaviour, so that's why they started building their own fortified settlements, called *longphuirt,* and fenced themselves off from the Irish tribes.

Up until then, the Irish had lived in scattered communities — there were no towns. The Vikings changed all that. In 841, they built a big longphort on the east coast near the small Irish settlement called Áth Cliath. This was to become a major trading centre and Ireland's first proper town. The deep water made a good harbour for the Viking ships. Their name for this place was 'Dubh Linn', which means 'black pool' (today's Dublin). Why? Because the merging waters of the Poddle and Liffey rivers were dark, having flowed through peat bogs, and black mud could be seen when the tide went out. More on Viking-age Dublin later on.

See how most of the Viking settlements are in the southern part of the country. It's not that the Vikings didn't like the north, it's just that a powerful tribe called the northern Uí Néill mostly kept them out.

DUBLIN

LIMERICK

WEXFORD

WATERFORD

CORK

Utterly sick of the Vikings' carry-on, the Irish tribes finally got their act together and had a series of battles over the next few years and gave the Vikings a right kicking. Part of the reason for this is that when the Vikings were attacking the monasteries, no one knew where they'd pop up. But when they started building longphuirt, the Irish could see where they were and went on the attack.

Irish warriors destroyed whole Viking communities in Meath, Cork and Kildare, killing hundreds of them. Even their biggest settlement at Dublin got attacked but not taken over. I wouldn't have liked to be a Viking in Ireland then!

40

Some Vikings left Ireland then but they liked the place too much so they came back. In fact, some Danish Vikings were later to come across from their settlements in England and started fighting with the Norwegian Vikings. The Irish fought against them both, but some Irish tribes decided they'd be better off joining forces with one side or the other. For instance, an Irish king called Áed Findliath joined forces with the Dublin Vikings to fight the High King of Ireland and with their help won the throne in 862.

So yeah, you could say that Ireland during the Viking age was a land at constant war. The Irish fought the Norwegian Vikings who fought the Danish Vikings who fought the Irish who fought themselves. There was a lot of fighting! But they didn't just shout names at each other (though they probably did that too!) so what did they use to do the fighting with?

STRIKING VIKINGS

WEAPONS AND BATTLES

If the Vikings had shopping catalogues where they could buy their weapons, they might have looked like this:

SALE NOW ON! PRICES SLASHED!

Long axe – swing this long-handled model hard with both hands to split skulls completely in two! Handles available up to 120 cm in length.

Skegg axe (bearded axe) – great for hooking over the rim of a shield or round an ankle! Short and long-handled versions available!

Hand axe – small and light, perfect to hide behind your shield for that nasty surprise! Can also be thrown to land right between the eyes!

Want something a bit flashier? Our talented blacksmiths can make axe-head designs in silver or gold for a superior hacking and slashing experience!

BUT HURRY – THIS SALE WON'T LAST FOREVER! *CHOP CHOP!*

FJORD SWORD

Suppliers of cutting-edge weapons since 793

Just back from raiding a monastery and have a few gold candlesticks to spare? Would you like to own a sword called 'Viper' or 'Flame of Battle'? How about 'Legbiter' or 'Wolf's Tooth'? Of course you would! Why wait to inherit a sword from your father when he kicks the bucket or hope your chief gives you one for loyal service?

Buy one from us to immediately raise your warrior status! Our skilled swordsmiths can make you a fine blade in just one year for the price of a good horse or a few cows.

Our swords are made using the latest *damascening* technology where heated iron bars are twisted together with lots of charcoal to make a tough, sharp, flexible blade. The blade is then *tempered* (strengthened) by heating it then quenching it in water, blood or urine. Of course, the best way to give your sword power is by killing lots of people with it. (When you pick up your new sword from us, you can test it out on one of our slaves for a small fee.)

Have your sword embossed with protective runes and the hilt decorated with magical symbols in silver filigree. We also make superior saxes (short swords), for the discerning Viking adventurer to hang on his belt.

NEW! Buy a quality leather scabbard lined with sheep-skin to keep your valuable sword in.

DON'T DELAY – BUY A SWORD FROM FJORD SWORD TODAY!

Only an idiot would rush into battle without a shield! And only a bigger idiot would use a shield not made by Shield-Maiden™!

Shield-Maiden™ shields are constructed according to the strictest rules! Light and robust, our shields can take a right proper batterin' from any Irish warrior!

WHERE YOU'RE THE BOSS!

- *core made of finest wood panels*
- *outer layer of superior rawhide*
- *your choice of leather or iron rim edging*
- *wood or iron handle riveted into place*
- *iron boss to deflect blows and protect your hand*
- *choose from hundreds of patterns with our exclusive shield-painting service*

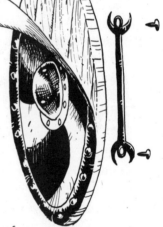

Sling your shield over the side of your ship to provide protection from arrows and spears AND to scare the bejapers out of your victims as you approach land!

Shield-Maiden™ shields can also be used as weapons! Smack your foes right in the mush or under the chin! ***TWAK!***

SPEAR CAMPAIGN

THE ONE-STOP SHOP
FOR ALL YOUR POINTY WEAPONS!

Don't have even enough cash for an axe? Then try our top-quality but very affordable spears and bows!

From light, perfectly balanced javelins to shorter thrusting spears and springy bows, we have a huge selection that will ensure you get your point across to your enemies!

Keep those sword-wielding Irish warriors out of slashing range with our long-shafted (2–3 m) spears. Crafted from the finest ash-wood, our spears come fitted with a leaf-shaped iron blade as standard for maximum armour penetration.

Their unique design means the rivet that holds the head to the shaft can be removed before throwing, so your enemy can't fire it right back at you! What proud Viking wants to be killed by his own spear?

The clever design has small wings either side of the blade so it doesn't get stuck too deep in your victim – perfect for easy removal!

Ideal for both doing battle and hunting dinner, our yew wood bows are made for optimum elasticity and strength.

Our arrows are made by the best fletchers and come with a range of heads – barbed ones for causing the nastiest wounds and narrower heads for penetrating chainmail and shields. Make sure you carry some of both in your quiver!

Viking warriors were the celebrities of their day. The deeds of a particularly magnificent warrior could be turned into a *skaldic* poem and retold many times over the years. This was the way the Vikings passed on information and knowledge, and like many newspapers and magazines of today, they sometimes didn't let the truth get in the way of a good story. But if magazines had been about back then, we might have seen covers like these:

Meet Helgi Half-Truth. As well as being a skaldic poet, he's a right storyteller. Which of his statements do you think are true? **Answers below.**

A) A BYRNIE CHAINMAIL SHIRT WEIGHS A WHOPPING 12 KILOS.

B) WE VIKINGS HAVE A NAME FOR THE TERRIFYING SOUND ARROWS MAKE – 'SKOTHRI'.

C) BOWS PERFORM BETTER WHEN THEIR STRINGS ARE WET.

D) WHEN VIKINGS DIE IN BATTLE THEY GO TO HEAVEN.

E) VIKINGS NAME THEIR AXES AFTER FEMALE TROLLS.

FIGHTING A BATTLE VIKING STYLE

From quick hit-and-run skirmishes to the famous shield-wall, the Vikings had a fighting style all their own. Said to have been given to the Vikings by the god Odin, one of the coolest tactics was called the *svinfylking* or 'boar formation'. It was used as a way to punch a hole through the enemy's battle lines.

The best warriors went right to the front, followed by the others in a big triangle. Interlocking their shields, they ran at the enemy like a wild boar charging. This smashed through the enemy's defences, taking them totally by surprise!

GNASH!
CHEW!

A special mention goes out to the Viking warriors known as *berserkers*. These were the craziest, fiercest fighters of all and were feared by both Vikings and Irishmen alike, as they were known to get so worked up they would kill whoever was in their way, friend or foe!

They were called berserkers after the Viking word for bear-skin because they often wore the hides of bears and other animals. They flew into battle foaming at the mouth, biting the edge of their shields and howling like wild animals. Kind of like your wee brother when you beat him in a game of air-hockey.

But hey – here we are talking about fighting and battles and berserkers and you don't really know anybody! How rude!

SLICE TO MEET YOU

VIKING NAMES

 VIKING NAME GENERATOR

1) Draw two circles on some card, one slightly bigger than the other, and cut them out.

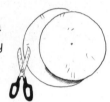

2) Write some names from column A on the list opposite around the edge of the bigger circle.

3) Then write some names from column B on the list around the edge of the smaller circle.

You can do one for boys and one for girls or mix them up for even more mad names.

4) Join the two circles in the centre with a paper fastener.

5) Decorate with runes (see page 89) or whatever Vikingy designs you like.

Now you've got yourself a Viking name generator! Close your eyes and turn the inner circle. Put your finger on the generator and then open your eyes! What's the first name you see? That's your Viking name!

BOYS

A	B
BJÖRN	THE STOUT
OLAF	SKULL-SPLITTER
SIGRID	THE RED
GORM	BLOODAXE
ARVID	HAIRY BREECHES
GUDRUN	LONG-NECK
EGIL	FOUL-FART
HELGI	FLAT-NOSE
ULF	FORKBEARD
SVEN	TROLL-BURSTER
RAGNAR	ILL-LUCK
ERIK	LEATHER-NECK
ORM	THE BONELESS
NJALL	THE SQUINT-EYED
SIGURD	SLENDER-LEG
THORSTEN	THE STINGY
IVAR	BERSERK-KILLER

GIRLS

A	B
ASTRID	THE BIG
BRYNHILD	RED-CHEEK
SIGRDIFA	THE FAIR
ALFDIS	DIRT-CHIN
SIV	THE CLUMSY
TURID	SECOND-SIGHTED
FREYA	MOSS-NECK
GUDRUN	THE TALL
SOLVEIG	THE GREAT ONE
GRIMHILD	THIN-LEGGED
VIGDIS	THE HAUGHTY
HILDUR	CRONE'S NOSE
SVANHILD	THE QUIET
INGRID	THE ELEGANT
HALLGERD	SCATTERBRAIN
RANVEIG	TANGLE-HAIR
TORHILD	THE DEEP-MINDED

QUICK- PULL MY FINGER!

I'M NOT FALLING FOR THAT AGAIN, IVAR!

Did you get a cool-sounding name like Thorsten Skullsplitter? Or something a bit silly like Ragnar Hairy Breeches? (That was a real Viking's name, by the way!) How about you, Astrid Tangle-Hair – have you found your comb yet? And just what have you been up to, Solveig Red-Cheek? (The less said about Ivar Foul-Fart, the better! Just don't get stuck in a lift with him!)

These were nicknames or *bynames* Vikings gave each other, and some were flattering and some were quite unkind. You got a nickname if you were a great fighter like Eric Bloodaxe, or had a remarkable physical feature, like Olaf Long-Neck, or were known for doing something such as Thorir the Troll-Burster. (Where he found the trolls to burst is anyone's guess!)

Some nicknames were given after the person had died, like poor Ottar the Vendel Crow who got his name when his body was eaten by crows after a battle at Vendel.

The Vikings had proper names as well. Boys were named after their fathers, so if your dad was called Sigurd and your name was Olaf, that made you Olaf, son of Sigurd and your name would be Olaf Sigurdson. (This is a bit like the 'Mc' and 'Mac' surnames we have in Ireland, which means 'son of'.) But *your* son Njall would be called Njall Olafson, or your daughter Ingrid would be called Ingrid Olafsdóttir.

Girls were named after their fathers, but sometimes also their mothers, like Astrid Hildursdóttir. So Viking people didn't have the same surname as their parents, which we might find a bit strange today.

Kids were often named after their ancestors – the Vikings thought that the dead relative's luck would attach to the child and bring them success throughout life.

Other times, kids were called after Norse gods and goddesses. Thor was very popular and so a lot of boys got names like Thorsten, Thorfast and Thorald and girls got called Freya a lot. Some were named after animals like Björn (bear), Orm (snake) or Ulf (wolf).

I CAN'T BE *THAT* LUCKY IF I'M *DEAD!*

In modern Ireland, surnames ending in -son or -sen are likely to have a Viking origin, like Thompson and Anderson. But there are other Viking/Irish surnames such as McAuliffe, which means 'son of Olaf' and McBirney, 'son of Björn' that aren't that obvious. These surnames would have come from a Viking family who changed the way they took names to be more like the Irish they were living among.

O'Loughlin and Higgins are both names that come from a word that means 'Viking'. The scroll on the next page has names on it that all have a Viking connection that is not as obvious as having a 'son' on the end.

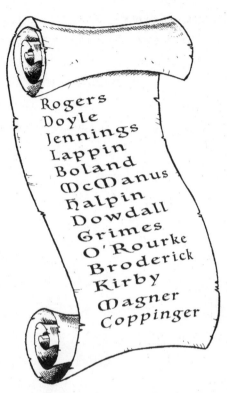

Rogers
Doyle
Jennings
Lappin
Boland
McManus
Halpin
Dowdall
Grimes
O'Rourke
Broderick
Kirby
Magner
Coppinger

Is your name on the list? (Mine definitely isn't. My surname Farrelly comes from the Irish *O'Faircheallaigh* which means 'descendant of Ferghal, the man of valour'. Ferghal was a leader of a tribe who fought with Brian Boru at the Battle of Clontarf *against* the Vikings. More on that later!)

Now you've got to know a few of their names, it's time to find out what the new Viking neighbours are like. Some of their ways are similar to the Irish ways and some are very strange indeed ...

LIKING BEING A VIKING

THEIR WAY OF LIFE

In 1974, workers digging foundations for offices at Wood Quay in Dublin discovered a whole Viking street.

Archaeologists saved what they could and much of the stuff they found is displayed in the National Museum in Dublin.

Visit the museum to see these things that are around 1,000 years old (just slightly younger than your granny). Listen carefully and you can almost hear the voices of the people who lived in Fishamble Street ...

IVAR! GET ME SOME MOSS TO WIPE MY BOTTOM!

Yes, it's true. Vikings did not have toilet roll or even old newspapers for *that* particular job. Useful stuff, moss! More on Viking-age Dublin later. Though they faced opposition from the native Irish, the Vikings set up homes in loads of places. They married Irish women and had their own families. Gradually, the two cultures became intertwined, a bit like the swirling dragons seen in both Viking and Irish art at the time.

BUILDING A VIKING HOUSE IN IRELAND

1) Hammer in four large wooden posts to hold up the roof.

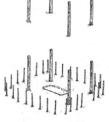

2) Put in a line of stakes where you want the walls to go.

3) Weave a *wattle* wall out of ash, hazel or willow saplings and wind it round the stakes. Add a second wattle wall and stuff the gap with moss and heather to keep in heat.

4) Make a sloping roof and cover it with straw thatch on top of grass sods. Leave a hole in it to let smoke out.

59

INSIDE AN IRISH VIKING HOUSE

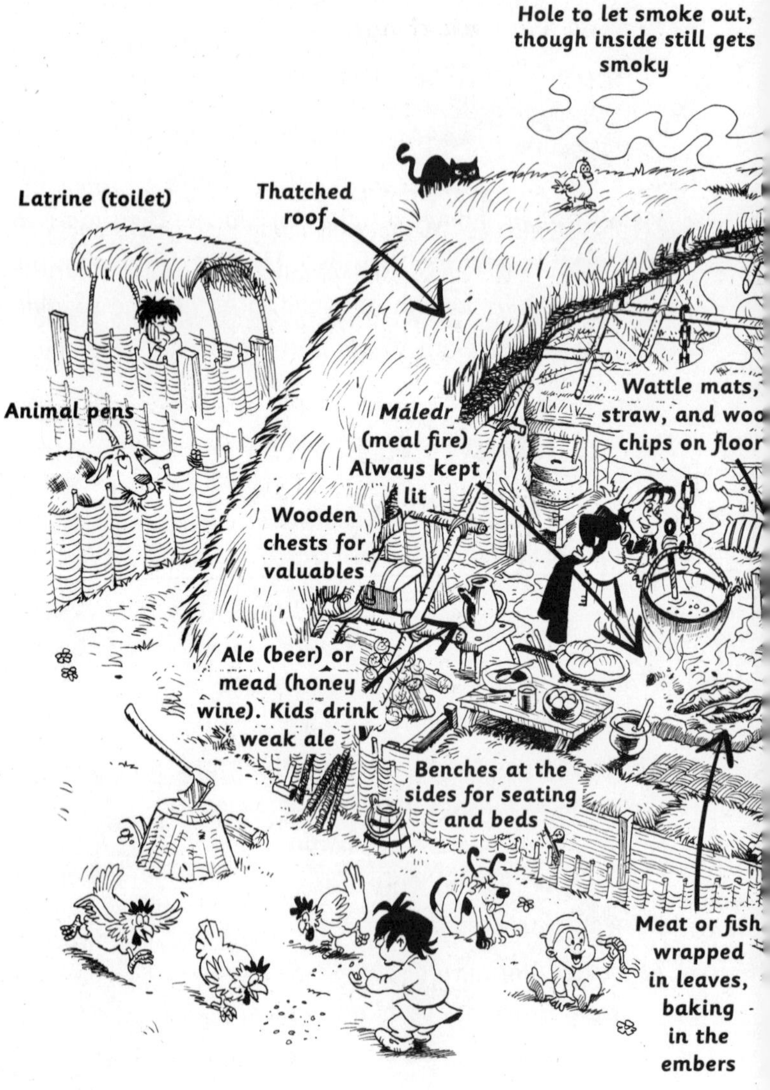

Hole to let smoke out, though inside still gets smoky

Latrine (toilet)

Thatched roof

Animal pens

Máledr (meal fire) Always kept lit

Wooden chests for valuables

Wattle mats, straw, and wood chips on floor

Ale (beer) or mead (honey wine). Kids drink weak ale

Benches at the sides for seating and beds

Meat or fish wrapped in leaves, baking in the embers

DEADLY! MEDLEY

Can you find these things?

☐ Weaving loom. Wool comes from the family's sheep. Clothes, blankets, tapestries and even ships' sails are made on the loom.

☐ An iron (made from heated glass) for pressing clothes. The board is made from whalebone.

☐ Tallow (animal fat) candles

☐ Tapestries to decorate the walls and keep heat in

☐ Weapon and shield display on wall

☐ Clay jugs and jars, all imported

☐ Soapstone bowl

☐ Quern-stone for grinding grain to make bread

☐ Rye or barley bread baking on skillets

☐ Iron or soapstone cooking pot

☐ Wooden bucket, bowl and plate.

☐ Metal knives and spoons but no forks — they haven't been invented yet!

☐ Cushions and furs

No windows

Food in sacks

Wattle walls

ANSWERS on page 143.

Apart from sheep, Viking families had other animals like cows, pigs and goats, to give milk, and chickens or geese for eggs. They also gathered nettles (you'll see why in a minute) and berries. Back in their own land of Scandinavia (and later, Iceland and Greenland) food sources would have been a lot different from those in Ireland. Vikings ate things like puffins, seals, horses, elks, and even bears!

They would also catch fish in rivers and lakes and at times, something even BIGGER!

DEADLY! VIKING RECIPES
HÁKARL — OR FERMENTED SHARK!

This is an old Viking dish that you can still get in Iceland (the country, not the shop) today!

All you need to do is catch a big Greenland shark, not one of those tiddlers you get in the sea around Ireland. But don't just cut it up and boil it — y'see, the Greenland shark's flesh is **poisonous!**

So to make the meat safe to eat, put the shark in a hole and cover it with sand and gravel. Then cover that with a pile of rocks for 6–12 weeks. This squeezes all the poisonous juices out of the flesh and then it starts to rot.

Simply dig up the rotten shark and hang it out to dry for a few months. Cut it up into small cubes and enjoy. Try not to gag while you're eating it but remember, the smell is much worse than the taste!

No sharks available? Then how about this tasty soup ...

NÄSSELSOPPA – OR NETTLE SOUP!

Serves 4

½ carrier bag of fresh nettle leaves, chopped (Don't forget to wear gloves when you're picking them, ya eejit!)

Chives, chopped

3 tbsp plain flour

1.5 litres (6 cups) of water

2 chicken or vegetable stock cubes (Vikings would have made their own stock)

2 hardboiled eggs

2 tbsp butter

salt and pepper

1) Rinse the nettle leaves in cold water to get rid of any creepy-crawlies – though you could leave those in for extra *crunch*!

2) Melt the butter, add the flour and stir. When golden, add the water, stock cubes, nettles and chives and boil for about 10 minutes.

3) Season with a little salt and pepper. Serve with half a boiled egg per portion.

Don't worry about this soup making you feel *prickly* – it's perfectly safe to eat!

A DEADLY! GUIDE TO ...
DRESSING LIKE A VIKING

What you *won't* need:

A HORNED HELMET Vikings never wore horns on their helmets. Horns would have made the helmet easier to knock off. They *may* have used a horned helmet in religious ceremonies.

A HUGE HAMMER The Norse god Thor did use a big hammer, but Vikings rarely used hammers as weapons.

ARMOUR Only wealthy Vikings wore armour and it didn't look anything like this!

FURRY PANTS Viking men didn't wear furry short pants; they wore trousers. One thing they didn't have – pockets. Vikings carried the stuff they needed in pouches on their belts.

BIG BOOTS Vikings wore simple leather shoes. In winter, they may have kept the fur on to keep their tootsies warm. Sometimes they wore wrappings around their lower legs to stop their trousers from getting torn.

65

What you will need:

BOYS

- A long-sleeved plain T-shirt a few sizes too big.
- A beach towel or table-cloth fastened at the shoulder with a brooch (see page 67 for how to make one).
- A belt. One from a dressing gown or judo suit will do.
- A pair of trackie bottoms or joggers. Tie strips of cloth or shoelaces round your lower legs.
- A pair of dark shoes or short boots.

GIRLS

- White headscarf or big handkerchief.
- Hair in braids.
- A plain-coloured long dress or you could use a long top.
- A long plain apron or a rectangle of cloth with a hole cut in it for your head.
- A pair of brooches pinned to the apron. See page 67 for how to make your own.
- A necklace of coloured beads strung between the brooches. See page 68 for how to make your own necklace.
- A pair of dark shoes or short boots.

DEADLY! CRAFTY VIKING BROOCH

To Make the Brooch

Viking girls wore two matching brooches.

1) Cut an oval disc out of a thick sheet of card.

2) Glue string in whatever pattern you want to the disc. You can also drop blobs of glue to make circles.

3) Once glue is dry, place face down on a sheet of tin foil, leaving about a 2-cm edge that you can fold over the edges of the disc. Glue or tape the edges down.

RUB RUB

4) Turn the disc over and gently rub the foil over the string to make the pattern stand out.

5) Paint the raised string area in a contrasting colour – gold or bronze metallic paint.

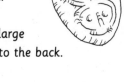

GOLD

6) Tape a large safety pin to the back.

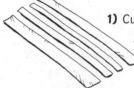

DEADLY! CRAFTY TO MAKE YOUR OWN BEADS

1) Cut out some thin strips of paper, about 20 cm long, making sure you vary the widths of the paper you use.

2) Put some glue over one side of each strip, then roll them up tight.

3) When glue is dry, paint the beads nice bright colours.

4) Thread the beads on a piece of string or cotton and tie the ends to the safety pins behind the brooch, then attach to your apron.

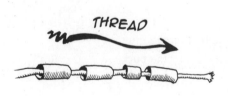

DEADLY! CRAFTY VIKING AXE

1) Take a sheet of cardboard measuring 25 x 50 cm. Put glue on one side of the sheet and roll it up tight lengthways. Leave to dry. This is the handle.

2) Get a sheet of thick card measuring 32 x 15 cm. Fold it in half lengthways. Draw the axe head shape onto the card, with the fold where the narrow end is. Cut out the axe head shape.

3) Glue the inside of the axe head to the end of the handle, and stick the two sides of the axe head together.

4) Paint the handle brown and draw some lines along it with a black marker to make it look more like wood.

5) Paint the axe head with silver paint. You can draw swirly patterns on it if you want.

DEADLY! CRAFTY VIKING SHIELD

1) Take two sheets of thick cardboard and draw a circle on each of them of about 60 cm in diameter. You can make a circle this big by tying a pencil to one end of a piece of string and the other end to a nail. Put the nail in the centre of the cardboard and draw out the circle. Cut them both out.

2) To make the boss (the bumpy bit in the centre of the shield): cut a 2-litre plastic bottle in half and make six equal cuts to the bottom half.

3) Draw a hole around the bottom of the bottle in the centre of one of the pieces of cardboard. Don't make the hole too big!

4) Cut out the hole. Push the bottle bottom through the hole in one of the pieces of circular card and bend over the cut plastic bits then tape or glue them to the cardboard. Then glue the other piece of circular card over the top of that.

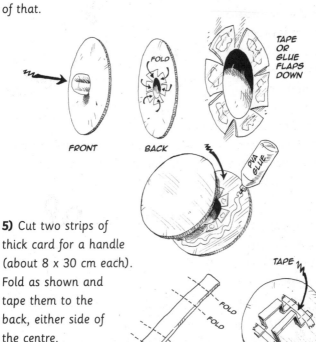

FRONT

BACK

FOLD

TAPE
OR
GLUE
FLAPS
DOWN

PVA GLUE

5) Cut two strips of thick card for a handle (about 8 x 30 cm each). Fold as shown and tape them to the back, either side of the centre.

FOLD
FOLD
FOLD
FOLD

TAPE

BACK

6) Paint the boss and the edge of the shield silver and the rest in the Viking style.

RED
YELLOW
SILVER

DEADLY! CRAFTY VIKING HELMET

1) Cut out three strips of thick card. One measuring 65 x 3 cm and the other two measuring 40 x 3 cm. Take the longest one and wrap it round your head, just above your eyebrows. Glue the ends together. This is the headband.

2) Mark the middles of the other two strips of card and glue together to form a cross shape.

3) Glue the ends of the cross shape inside the headband.

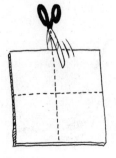

4) Take a sheet of card and cut out 4 pieces, 1.5 cm bigger than the spaces between the cross shape and the headband.

5) Glue the sheets into the inside of the helmet.

6) Insert paper fasteners into different points on the cross shape and headband. Use some tape to stick the ends down so they don't stick into your head, doofus!

7) Measure the space between your eyes. Draw two dots onto a sheet of card that distance apart, then draw eye-shaped holes around them.

8) Draw the rest of the eyepiece shape like the grey area here. Then cut out the eye-holes. Glue the eyepiece to the outside of the headband. You can draw fierce 'eyebrows' on the eyepiece if you want.

9) Paint the whole lot with silver paint. Voilà! Your own Viking helmet. (Just don't try stopping an axe blow with it though!)

73

This is Brynhild Truth-Twister. She spins yarns as much as she weaves wool! Which of her statements do you think are true? **Answers below.**

A) VIKING WOMEN WORK FOR 14 HOURS OR LONGER EVERY DAY.

B) VIKING CHILDREN GO TO SCHOOL.

C) VIKING MEN AND WOMEN MARRY FOR LOVE.

D) VIKING WOMEN CAN'T GET DIVORCED FROM THEIR HUSBANDS.

E) VIKING PEOPLE ARE REALLY DIRTY AND SMELLY.

Answers below.

ANSWERS: Brynhild is such a liar! She managed to tell the truth only once! a) *True* – Viking women worked very hard preparing food, cooking, weaving, brewing, sewing, cleaning, spinning, baking AND she did her husband's jobs when he was away. b) *Nope, no school!* HOORAY! Viking kids stayed home all day, but BOO! They had loads of chores to do. c) *Afraid not.* Most Viking marriages were arranged by the marrying families. Fathers of the bride got a 'bride-price' from the groom. d) *Untrue.* They could divorce a man who was cruel by stating it in front of witnesses. e) *False!*

74

Vikings were well-known for their cleanliness. Their name for Saturday was *Laugardagr* which means 'washing day' when they had a bath and cleaned their clothes. This was a lot more than many people living at the same time! They also washed every day. They made their own soap from – guess what? Chestnuts!

Vikings carried combs for their hair and beards, tweezers for plucking eye-brows and picks for cleaning their nails. They even had little ear spoons for scooping out ear-wax!

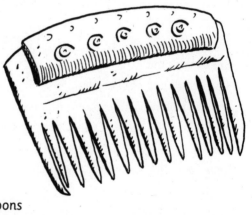

What happened if you got sick in Viking times? Let's find out!

ONE-EYED HELGA'S
DEADLY! HEALING TIPS*

Aww, you've been butted by the family goat and broken your arm, have you? No problem. I'll just spread an ointment made from daisies and egg whites on it and set the bone straight. Well, as straight as I can make it anyway! I've only got one eye, you know! HEH, HEH, HEH! NEXT!

So you've got an arrow in your belly, have you? I have the perfect thing for that!

Here, take some of my lovely leek and herb broth before you lie down. What do you mean you don't feel like eating? Get it into you! I have to find out if the arrowhead has made a hole in your stomach or not! If the wound smells of leeks and herbs, then it definitely has!

SNIFF, SNIFF! Oooh, not good news, I'm afraid! I can smell something leeky which means YOU'RE leaky! You'll soon be goin' on a one-way trip to Valhalla!

Stories of Viking healers can be found in their sagas.

HEH, HEH, HEH! NEXT!
Hello, dear! What seems to be the problem? Ah, I see – your guts are all hanging out from a sword wound. Not to worry – I'll just fill the wound with cobwebs to stop the bleeding and scoop your entrails back in. Then I'll sew you up. The bad news is the needle isn't very sharp. The good news is, the thread is made from silk! Fancy, very fancy! Eh? No, you won't be asleep during the agonising procedure, don't be silly. If you're still alive in the next few weeks, the operation was a great success. If you die, it wasn't. HEH, HEH, HEH! NEXT!

Hello, my lovely! What's the matter with you? You've pricked your finger with a rose thorn? It's going to have to come off, I'm afraid ...

Now we know a little more about the Viking neighbours. Let's find out what the kids are like ...

BJÖRN & FREYA

VIKING KIDS AND FAMILIES

Viking kids may not have had to go to school, but they didn't sit around playing video games and watching telly. I *could* tell you what they did get up to on a typical day, but I'll let 12-year-old Freya and 10-year-old Björn tell it their way ...

Björn's Diary: Slept like a log last night but got kicked awake before cock's crow by Freya who had a face on her like a wolfhound chewing a wasp. She's never any fun these days!

Freya's Diary: My pesky little toe-rag of a brother Björn snored all night so I hardly got any sleep. It's not like I haven't got a full day's work ahead of me! When did he become sooooo annoying?

B: Did my usual first job of the day — stoking the fire back to life so Mum could make breakfast. I'm pretty good at the old fire-minding business, if I do say so myself! I made Granny giggle by pretending to be the thunder-god Thor, firing lightning bolts from the sky! YAAAAR!

F: Björn got off to his usual noisy start by chucking a few logs on the fire. Big deal! It's not like he's even any good at fire-minding - he's always letting it go out! I had to fetch water from the well and milk the cows while he was doing his stupid Thor impression. Why Granny finds it so funny, I'll never know.

B: After breakfast (porridge AGAIN!) Freya spent even longer than usual combing her hair — like anybody's looking at her! I had to split logs, gather eggs and feed the chickens. Dad says later on he'll show me how to kill one of the older chickens so we can have it for dinner. It's not laying as many eggs as it used to so it's only good for meat. Can't wait!

F: Didn't get to spend as long on my hair as I usually do as Mum wanted me to grind grain on the quern-stone (I HATE that job!). What if Magnus Ulfson sees the state of me? He's soooo dreamy. *SIGH!* Heard Dad telling Björn he'd show him how to kill a chicken later. Guess who'll have to pluck the flipping thing?! Mum will want the feathers to stuff a mattress for the new baby. (*Please, please, please*, Odin, let it be a girl!)

B: I just know the new baby is going to be a boy! I've prayed to Odin enough times. He wouldn't give me another stinky sister ... would he? Mum's lost two babies already so hopefully this one will be okay.

And I've been praying to Mum's Christian God too, just in case. (Mum is Irish but my Dad's from Norway.) Dad is teaching me to be a wood carver like him and he's letting me carve a toy bear (my name means 'bear') for my baby BROTHER in his workshop, but only after I get my chores done. I'm nearly finished it!

F: Churning butter, kneading dough, brewing ale, beating flax, combing wool, ironing, spindling, winding yarn ... while Björn learns to be a carver, I have *tons* of boring chores to do! How's that fair?! I know he does chores too, but he gets to mess about in Dad's workshop all day making a duck (or is it a rabbit?). On the upside, Mum is letting me help her weave a blanket for my new baby *SISTER* on the loom. I don't know if I'll ever get the hang of it.

B: Hate to admit it, but Freya is getting pretty good on the loom. I wouldn't mind a go on it as it looks like fun, but Dad says it's woman's work. Ah well! After we had some bread, cheese, apples and ale at midday, Dad continued my warrior training by teaching me how

to fight with a wooden sword and a kid-size shield. He never lets me win but that's because he says I have to learn how to fight as our enemies wouldn't let me win either.

I also practised some spear-throwing and just missed Magnus Ulfson's head! I didn't mean to but he took it thick and came over and punched me in the eye.

Dad let him because he said it was his right. I did nearly skewer him, I suppose, but he is 13 and I'm only 10. I HATE Magnus Ulfson.

F: Ohhhh, I LOVE Magnus Ulfson!

82

B: Swept up and bagged the wood shavings and sawdust from the workshop (people buy it from us for covering their floors) and then worked on my bear carving a bit more. Before I could go and play with my best friend Erik, I had to feed the pigs, split more logs and get the fire hot for dinner. Dad showed me how to kill the chicken but it was a bit of a disappointment - you just snap its neck. No blood or anything. But YAAAY! Chicken for dinner!

Freya's not talking to me since she found out I nearly harpooned her boyfriend. Suits me. All she talks is nonsense these days anyway!

F: I can't believe that little freak Björn almost killed my poor darling Magnus!!! If he'd died, I would never have had a chance to kiss those sweet, pink rosebud lips!

B: What a laugh me and Erik had! We played at *Glima* — Viking wrestling! It can get a bit rough sometimes. I ripped Erik's trousers by accident and you could see his butt through the tear.

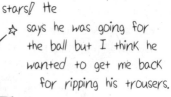

Then we played a quick game of *Knattleikr* with some of the other lads. Erik hit me such a wallop with his *Knattgildra* stick that I saw stars! He

says he was going for the ball but I think he wanted to get me back for ripping his trousers.

F: While that little monster was out playing, I had to pluck a chicken! Not only that, but Mum insisted on teaching me how to cook it. We cut off the head and ripped out the guts - which Mum will use for soup - then rubbed it in melted butter and salt and stuffed it with some herbs from our garden. Then we wrapped it in leaves, put it in a skillet with some water and left it over hot embers to cook. The whole time I imagined it was Björn.

B: Before dinner, me and Dad played a game of Hnefatafl on a nice board Dad carved himself. He carved the playing pieces as well. Dad beats me at it most of the time but I have won a few games. You have to defend the king while your opponent tries to capture him. Dad says Glima and Knattleikr are important games that will strengthen my body but Hnefatafl is a game of wits and cunning that will best prepare me for life.

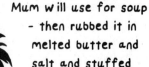

F: Björn gets to play Hnefatafl while I have to finish the chicken off on the spit to make the skin crispy. No fair! Still, Mum says that chores are important as they make me strong for when I have my own children, and cooking for my family is a skill that will best prepare me for life.

B: It's a long time since I enjoyed dinner so much! BURRRPP! Freya made most of it. How could my horrible sister make such a nice meal? At least she's talking to me again. I think she felt a bit sorry for me when she saw the black eye Magnus OAF-son gave me. Before bed, Dad told a few stories about the gods (the one about Thor at the wedding is my favourite) and played some tunes on his jaw-harp. Granny sang some sad songs in Irish which made me cry a teeny bit. I couldn't help myself! I hope Freya didn't notice but I let on I was laughing just in case. Before we blew out the candles, I finished my bear!

F: That dinner was great even if I say so myself! We can use the chicken carcass and giblets for soup for tomorrow night's dinner. I felt a little bad for my pain-in-the-backside brother when I saw his eye all half-closed and purple. He didn't mean to nearly gore Magnus to death, after all. I saw him wiping tears from his cheeks when Granny was singing her beautiful, sad songs but he just pretended to be laughing. He's finished his wood carving at last. I'm sure our little sister - or brother - will love the dragon (or is it a horse?!) he made.

I'm happy to report that Björn and Freya's Mum had twins! A boy and a girl! They got Irish names this time – Amhlaoibh and Bláthnaid.

And Björn got to carve another bear/duck/rabbit/dragon/horse!

TRY NOT TO RUNE YOUR DAY
THE FUTHARK

Although many Vikings couldn't read or write, they still had a system of letters or runes called the *Futhark*. They believed runes possessed magical qualities and each one had a different magical meaning.

You probably don't realise it, but even the letters we use every day are a bit magical. They are, after all, symbols for the sounds words make. That's why we 'spell' words, like in a magic spell. Also, our word 'grammar' comes from the word *grimoire* which means 'spell book'. So when you write something down you are kind of casting a magic spell. Cool, eh?

Vikings believed that the god Odin discovered runes after he sacrificed an eye to drink from *Mimir*, the well of knowledge. Then he hung from the great tree *Yggdrasil* for nine nights. After that, he went a

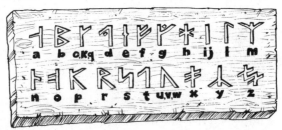

bit mad and started carving runes into everything he could lay his hands on: trees, chariot wheels, shields and even the teeth of his eight-legged horse, *Sleipnir*. More about Odin in the next chapter.

The number of runes in the runic alphabet changed over time – the Vikings sometimes used as many as 33 and sometimes only 16. This is what a 21-rune Futhark looks like:

All the symbols are in straight lines (like the ancient Irish Ogham alphabet) because straight lines are easier to carve on wood, stone and leather than curved ones. The Vikings didn't use paper, y'see.

Try writing your name using these runes then translate the messages below. **Answers below.**

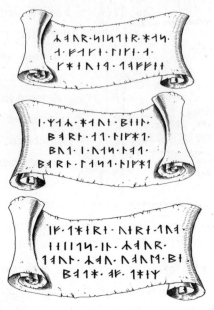

The Vikings (those who could write anyway) carved their names on their belongings — swords, bowls and jewellery — same  as how you might write your name on your pencil case. There's a deer antler in the National Museum in Dublin with a helpful runic inscription that says, 'deer antler'.

ANSWERS: *Your sister has a face like a chewed toffee. I may have been born at night but I was not born last night. If there were two eejits in your town you would be both of them.*

90

One other use the runes had was telling the future. Travelling fortune tellers would get paid to 'cast the runes' for people. Each rune was inscribed on a stone and thrown a certain way. The fortune teller then told the person's future from the way the runestones fell.

Runes were not only used for magical purposes. There is a marble bannister in a church in Turkey with runes scratched into it that say, 'Halfdan Was Here.' This ancient graffiti was probably carved by a bored Viking warrior during a church service!

Let's find out a bit more about the stories the Vikings told, their myths and legends and the gods they worshipped. Get ready to be amazed!

YOU RAGNARÖK MY WORLD

MYTHS AND LEGENDS

You might know some of the gods and goddesses the Vikings worshipped and told stories about from films, comics and video games, but the Norse gods were even stranger than you can imagine.

THE AXE FILES

ODIN

NAME: ODIN

ALIASES: THE ALLFATHER, WODEN, KING OF THE AESIR, GOD OF WAR, OL' ONE-EYE

KNOWN ASSOCIATES: GODDESS FRIGG (WIFE), THE RAVENS HUGIN & MUNIN (THOUGHT & MEMORY), SLEIPNIR, AN EIGHT-LEGGED HORSE

DISTINGUISHING FEATURES: ONLY HAS ONE EYE. OFTEN DISGUISED AS AN OLD MAN WITH A FLOPPY HAT. PRETTY MUCH ALL-POWERFUL

WEIRD RATING: 💀💀💀💀

THOR

NAME: THOR

ALIASES: SON OF ODIN, GUARDIAN OF ASGARD, GOD OF THUNDER, HAMMER BOY

KNOWN ASSOCIATES: HIS MAGIC HAMMER MJOLLNIR

DISTINGUISHING FEATURES: STRONG, MUSCULAR, HANDSOME, HATES GIANTS AND TROLLS, NOT VERY BRIGHT, LOVES FIGHTING

WEIRD RATING:

ELLI

NAME: ELLI

ALIASES: GODDESS OF OLD AGE, SUPERGRAN

KNOWN ASSOCIATES: NONE

DISTINGUISHING FEATURES: SHE'S A REALLY OLD LADY, BUT SHE ONCE BEAT THOR IN A WRESTLING MATCH. EVEN HE CAN'T DEFEAT OLD AGE

WEIRD RATING:

FREYA

NAME: FREYA

ALIASES: GODDESS OF LOVE,
BEAUTY AND FERTILITY, YUMMY MUMMY

KNOWN ASSOCIATES: GOD NJORD,
FATHER; GOD FREYR, TWIN BROTHER

DISTINGUISHING FEATURES: RIDES A CHARIOT PULLED BY BIG
BLUE CATS, COLLECTS SOULS OF FALLEN WARRIORS, BEST-LOVED
OF THE NORSE GODDESSES

WEIRD RATING:

LOKI

NAME: LOKI

ALIASES: GOD OF MISCHIEF,
LORD OF LIES, BAD LAD

KNOWN ASSOCIATES: HIS CHILDREN
JORMUNGAND THE WORLD SERPENT,
SLEIPNIR THE HORSE, FENRIR THE GIANT
WOLF AND HEL, THE RULER OF THE DEAD.
THAT'S ONE STRANGE FAMILY!

DISTINGUISHING FEATURES: SHAPE-SHIFTING ABILITY, ALWAYS UP
TO NO GOOD, LIKES A GOOD LAUGH AT THE EXPENSE OF OTHERS.
BEST AVOIDED!

WEIRD RATING:

94

You can trust the god Loki about as far as you can throw him. Which of his statements do you think are true? **Answers below.**

A) THOR HAS TWO GOATS THAT PULL HIS CHARIOT. SOMETIMES HE EATS THEM BUT BRINGS THEM BACK TO LIFE THE NEXT DAY.

B) ODIN OWNS A GOLD RING THAT MAKES EIGHT COPIES OF ITSELF EVERY NINTH NIGHT.

C) I ONCE CUT OFF THE GODDESS SIF'S BEAUTIFUL GOLDEN HAIR WHEN SHE WAS SLEEPING, JUST FOR A LAUGH!

D) FRIDAY IS NAMED AFTER THE VIKING GODDESS OF WISDOM.

E) VIKINGS BELIEVE THE COSMOS IS HELD IN PLACE BY A GIANT ASH TREE CALLED YGGDRASIL.

ANSWERS: Loki may like to make mischief, but he wasn't lying! At least not this time ... a) True! They were called Toothgnasher and Toothgrinder. b) Yep! It was a ring called Draupnir made for him by dwarves. c) Uh-huh. Cruel as it was, Loki did this. The dwarves made Sif some new hair though. d) True. Friday is named after Frigg who was Odin's wife and the goddess of wisdom, love, beauty and knowledge. Other days of the week are named after Norse gods too. More on that later! e) Oooh yeah! In fact, it wasn't just giant, it was absolutely HUMONGOUS!

YGGDRASIL & THE NINE WORLDS

Máni

Asgard
Realm of Aesir gods

Sol

Alfheim
Realm of Light Elves

Vanaheim
Realm of Vanir gods

Midgard
Realm of Men

Svartalfheim
Realm of Dwarves

Muspelheim
Realm of
Fire Giants

Jotunheim
Realm of Giants

Helheim
Realm of
Lost Souls

Niflheim
Realm of
Ice & Mists

At the centre of the Viking universe is the great tree, Yggdrasil. Within its roots and branches lie the nine worlds of gods, men, dwarves, elves and giants.

ASGARD – kingdom of the high gods known as the Aesir, ruled over by Odin

VANAHEIM – home to the old gods, the Vanir

ALFHEIM – realm of the light elves

MIDGARD – the human world, surrounded by Jormungand, the World Serpent

SVARTALFHEIM – underground home of the dwarves

JOTUNHEIM – home of the frost and stone giants where king Thrym rules

MUSPELHEIM – domain of the fire giants, ruled by Surt

NIFLHEIM – a barren land of fog and ice

HELHEIM – land of the dead, ruled by Hel

At the top of the tree sits the Great Eagle (no-one knows his name) and in its roots lives Nidhogg the dragon. The Eagle and Nidhogg hate each other and a squirrel called Ratatosk passes messages between them all day. He likes to cause trouble by making stuff up.

A rainbow bridge called Bifrost spans the gap between Asgard and Midgard. It is guarded all the time by the watchman, Heimdall.

HAVE SOME HÁVAMÁL

The god Odin gave the Vikings practical advice to live by, which they wrote down and called the *Hávamál*. It's not exactly a barrel of laughs, but here is Allfather Odin himself spouting some of his wonderful wisdom...

> 'BEFORE YOU ENTER A HOUSE, CHECK ALL THE CORNERS BECAUSE YOU NEVER KNOW WHERE ENEMIES MIGHT BE HIDING.'

Great advice, especially if you're playing a zombie video game!

> 'YOU SHOULD KNOW HOW MANY LOGS TO STOCK IN AUTUMN SO YOU HAVE ENOUGH WOOD FOR YOUR WINTER FIRE.'

In other words, BE PREPARED!

> 'IF YOU STARE AT SOMETHING YOU DROPPED ON THE GROUND FOR LONG ENOUGH, EVENTUALLY SOMEONE WILL PICK IT UP FOR YOU.'

Okay, I made that last one up. But it's still good advice and has worked for me many times!

PARTY TIME

The Vikings had no TV or internet (heck, they didn't even have BOOKS!) so they entertained themselves by telling stories. It didn't take much for a Viking chief to throw a party but when he did, he hired professional poets called *skalds* to entertain his guests. The skald would tell stories called *sagas*, but he was also expected to make up poems praising the chief who threw the party or he might be the one who ended up *scalded!*

THERE WAS THIS CHIEFTAIN CALLED SVEN
WHO THOUGHT HE WAS THE BRAVEST OF MEN
BUT HE ONCE SAW A MOUSE
INSIDE HIS LONGHOUSE
WHO MADE HIM RUN AWAY LIKE A HEN!

These poems would recount the brave deeds of the chief and his warriors, how they travelled the seas in search of adventure, treasure and slaves!

A skald couldn't just tell the tale in a straightforward way like when your big brother writes a story for his homework.

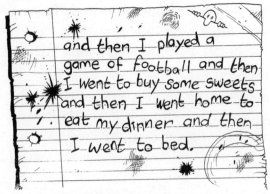

and then I played a game of football and then I went to buy some sweets and then I went home to eat my dinner and then I went to bed.

... because that's **BORRRR-ING!** A skald poet used words that made ordinary things sound fantastic! These were called *kennings* and were usually two or three-word phrases. A skilled skald could make your brother's story sound like this:

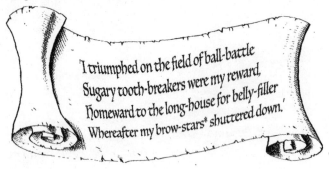

'I triumphed on the field of ball-battle
Sugary tooth-breakers were my reward,
Homeward to the long-house for belly-filler
Whereafter my brow-stars* shuttered down.'

*eyes

Okay, it's not Shakespeare, but at least it's better than your brother's effort!

So in Viking poetry, the wind is a 'breaker of trees', the sea is a 'whale's road' and warriors are 'children of battle.'

What do you think some of these kennings are? **Answers below.**

1) Battle-sweat
2) War needles
3) Sleep story
4) Sky-candle
5) Foam horse

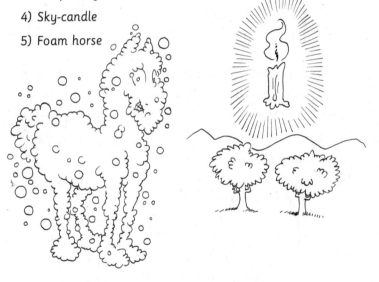

Now try writing your own! Think up kennings for these things: cat, baby sister, car, new trainers, birthday party, dog, best friend, shark, teacher. Let your imagination run riot!

ANSWERS: 1) Blood 2) Arrows 3) A dream 4) The sun 5) A ship.

A VIKING BESTIARY*

Here are just a few of the mythological 'Hidden Folk' you might encounter in the realms beyond the human world.

JORMUNGAND – The world serpent. He's rather large, able to surround the entire world.

STRENGTHS: **He's rather large, able to surround the entire world!**

WEAKNESSES: If he comes out of the sea, it will bring about *Ragnarök* – the end of the world!

FENRIR – Fenrir is a ferocious gigantic wolf who is so strong he breaks every iron chain that binds him.

STRENGTHS: Incredible size and strength.

WEAKNESSES: A chain called *Gleipnir* made from the sound of a cat's footsteps, the beard of a woman, the roots of a mountain, the sinews of a bear, the breath of a fish, and the spittle of a bird.

TROLLS – Trolls come in all shapes and sizes but they are always slow, ugly, dim-witted creatures.

STRENGTHS: Trolls are very strong, love eating humans and have a great sense of smell.

WEAKNESSES: Big billy goats. They also hate iron and will turn to stone if exposed to daylight.

JÖTNAR – These ice giants are unfriendly, violent beings.

STRENGTHS: Some Jötnar are quite clever and love a good riddle.

WEAKNESSES: A big hair-dryer.

DRAUGAR – Viking zombies. Flesh-eating, blood-drinking ghouls who guard their treasure-filled graves.

STRENGTHS: Very strong, can increase size, turn into smoke and 'swim' through solid rock.

WEAKNESSES: They smell really bad!

KRAKEN – This massive squid-like creature is often mistaken for an island.

STRENGTHS: Able to crush a ship and pull it under the waves.

WEAKNESSES: A good sushi chef.

*a bestiary is a book of beasts

Vikings believed they went to Odin's great hall Valhalla when they died honourably in war. Their souls were reaped from the battlefields by warrior-women called Valkyries. They then spent their days killing each other and resurrecting to have a great feast every night. Not my idea of heaven, but hey, I'm not a Viking!

When rich, powerful Vikings died they were buried in a longship with all their belongings – sometimes even their slaves and pets were killed and sent along with them! There are also stories of the longships being set alight and adrift on the sea. Other Vikings were buried in graves marked out with stones in the shape of a ship.

The end of the Viking world will be *Ragnarök* when most of the gods fight a whopping great battle to the death, like a lethal wrestling smackdown. Odin, Thor, Loki, Freya ... all will die. Even the Viking gods cannot escape death. (Though I've always wondered, if they already know it's gonna happen, can't they, like, just not do it? Just sayin'!)

THE THING IS ...

LAW AND PUNISHMENT

If you reckon a Viking Thing looked something like this ...

... you would be very mistaken! The Vikings called their important meetings or assemblies *Things*. Here they created laws (the word 'law' is actually a Viking word), decided arguments and judged criminals. This would go on for several days, so they also had fun in between all the serious stuff. Though what the Vikings called 'fun' we might call 'dangerous'! Once a year, there was the *Althing* in Iceland, where the really important stuff was decided, like the election of a new chief or king. (If nobody turned up, was it called a *No-thing*?)

105

Dublin Vikings had a big meeting called a Thingmote on a mound south of the River Liffey, near where College Green is today. We don't know for sure what went on there as the Vikings never wrote anything down, but a programme for a typical Thing might've looked like this:

DUBLIN THINGMOTE
ALL FREEMEN AND THEIR FAMILIES WELCOME!

7.30am – Breakfast of ale, porridge and bread.

8.30am – Call to assembly by horn-blowers. Welcome address by the chief, Jarl Thorstein Skull-Splitter.

9am – Opening speech by the Law-Speaker who recites all the laws he knows by heart.

9.30am – Judgement upon Olaf Flat-Nose who stands accused of smiting Knut the Witless with a heavy stone, leaving him with addled brains. Olaf will face *jernbyrd* (trial by ordeal) to determine his guilt.

He will have to snatch hot iron from boiling water and carry it for nine paces. If he drops it, he's guilty!

Suggested punishments for Olaf, if found guilty: declared an outlaw and banished from the land,* payment of a *mulct* (fine) or being smitten with a heavy stone until he himself is left with addled brains.

11am – Break for some horse-fighting! Place your bets!

12pm – *Holmgang* (duel) between Oleg Big-Mouth and Snorri the Boastful because Oleg said Snorri's wife Hildur had a face like the back end of a horse. The loser is the man whose blood hits the ground first. Bring some sandwiches.

1.30pm – Swimming competition. Not so much swimming as holding your opponent underwater until he drowns or gives up. Great fun!

Banishment doesn't sound too bad, but then anyone is allowed to kill you without being punished. Better run!

2.30pm – More horse fighting!

3.30pm – Judgement upon Finni the Squint-Eyed who stands accused of stealing Erik the Foul-Tempered's

goat. Finni swears the goat was won fair and square when he beat Erik in a Hnefatafl game but there are no witnesses to this. All freemen will vote to decide who owns the goat and the loser will have to pay the winner another goat on top.

4.30pm – Glima wrestling match. The winner is the first man to smash his opponent over a big rock.

6pm – Dinner feast. Veal stew, wild pig, roast sheep and spit-roasted venison. Bring your own mead. **Skol!***

After-dinner entertainment: Music by *Ragnar Rock and the Berserkers* who will perform their Number One hit *'I Dreamed a Dream.'***

* Skol is Viking for 'cheers!' or 'sláinte!'

**Only one fragment of a Viking song has ever been found and this was the title.

This is Rusla the Red Maiden*, who not only has a reputation for being terribly bloodthirsty, but also for being a big fat liar. Which of her statements do you think are true? **Answers below.**

A) IF YOU COMMIT A CRIME IN VIKING TIMES, YOU GET SENT TO PRISON.

C) A VIKING CALLED RAGNAR LODBROK WAS EXECUTED BY BEING THROWN INTO A PIT OF SNAKES.

D) A VIKING CAN GET AWAY WITH MURDERING ANOTHER VIKING IF THEY KEEP QUIET ABOUT IT.

B) ONE TERRIBLE VIKING PUNISHMENT IS THE BLOOD-EAGLE. CUT OPEN A MAN'S BACK, FOLD OUT HIS RIBS AND TAKE HIS LUNGS OUT WHILE HE'S STILL ALIVE!

ANSWERS: a) Nope! The Vikings didn't have prisons. b) True! Also, salt was rubbed in the wounds to make it more agonising. c) Yep! He was executed by an English king called Aella. His sons avenged his death by invading England. d) False. For a Viking to get away with killing another Viking, he had to do it during the day, preferably in front of people, state publicly why he did it, then pay a fine to the dead person's family. There was no punishment for killing non-Vikings.

* Rusla actually existed. She was a Viking warrior-princess who loved a good scrap. The sagas tell of how she went to war after someone insulted her brother! She also fought at the Battle of Clontarf.

As well as passing laws, judging crimes and making decisions, the Thing was a great time for old friends to meet up and share gossip. Also, Dublin was a thriving Viking trading centre and traders from all over the known world came to the Thing to sell their wares.

TRADING POST

CARRIER SACKS - 1 HACKSILVER EXTRA

WHETSTONES

SOAPSTONE

FURS

CLOTH

FEATHERS

AMBER

SALT

IRON

WALRUS IVORY

TIN

Stuff like ...

Amber – used for making jewellery

Soapstone – to make cooking pots

Cloth – wool and silk

Tin – to mix with copper to make bronze. Also used to cover bronze to make it look like silver. Sneaky!

Walrus ivory – to make art and carvings

Feathers – to stuff mattresses

Furs – to make warm clothing

Iron – loads of uses, but mostly making weapons

Whetstones – to sharpen blades

Salt – to preserve meat and fish

And of course, SLAVES! Dublin was a major slave-trading port and female Irish slaves were highly prized.

It's thought that Viking society couldn't have survived without slaves, or *thralls* as the Vikings called them. Thralls did all the backbreaking or disgusting jobs but they weren't treated very well. They had few legal rights and were seen as property – not people – worth just a few cows. The good news is if somebody killed a thrall, their owner could go to the Thing to get compensation. (Hey, I didn't say it was good news for the *thrall!*)

So we've seen what the Thingmote at Dublin was like and how Vikings dealt with wrongdoers. But what about the rest of Dublin? As Ireland's biggest Viking town, a lot of things happened there. Let's find out what in the latest episode of ... *Fishamble Street*.

FISHAMBLE STREET

A VIKING (SOAP) OPERA

Archaeologists found tons of stuff when the Wood Quay area of Dublin was dug up by builders. Most of it ended up in the National Museum in Dublin. See if you can find these things in this episode of Fishamble Street. Good luck finding them all! **Answers on page 144**.

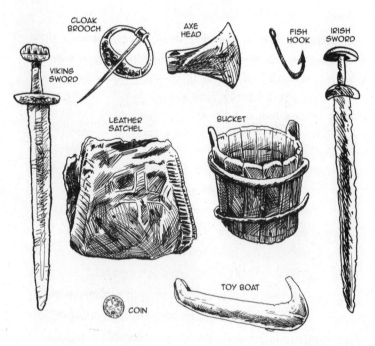

CLOAK BROOCH

AXE HEAD

FISH HOOK

IRISH SWORD

VIKING SWORD

LEATHER SATCHEL

BUCKET

TOY BOAT

COIN

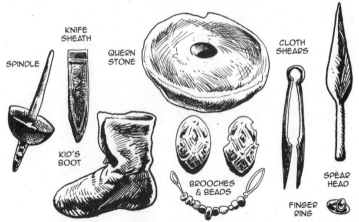

SPINDLE

KNIFE
SHEATH

QUERN
STONE

CLOTH
SHEARS

KID'S
BOOT

BROOCHES
& BEADS

FINGER
RING

SPEAR
HEAD

FISHAMBLE · STREET

113

114

115

116

117

118

119

120

DID YOU FIND ALL THE OBJECTS FROM THE MUSEUM? ANSWERS ON PAGE 144.

NEXT TIME ON

ULF AND ORM FALL OUT OVER A BURIED TREASURE HOARD AND OLAF MEETS A GIRL.

I ONLY WANTED TO AXE YOU SOMETHING

THE BATTLE OF CLONTARF

EVERYBODY has heard of Brian Boru. If you hadn't, you have now. He is a legend in Ireland, kind of like its first superhero.

I THINK YOU'LL FIND *CÚ CHULAINN* IS IRELAND'S FIRST SUPERHERO!

NO *WAY! FIONN MAC CUMHAILL* IS!

AHEM! HANG ON THERE NOW, LADS ...

But the things we most associate with him – the unification of Ireland, the harp, the end of the Viking age in Ireland – were all added much later by the Christian monks who were known to exaggerate a bit. They wanted to make the Battle of Clontarf all about the struggle between good and evil, but it was much more complicated than that.

If modern-day merchandise had been around back in the 11th century, we may have seen stuff like this:

BRIAN BORU ACTION FIGURE

Accessories include sword, spear, shield and giant gold cross.*

SAYS 4 PHRASES:

1. YAAAAAARRR!

2. I AM KING OF IRELAND!

3. GET OUT OF MY LAND, YOU DIRTY, STINKIN' VIKINGS!

4. COME OUT AND FACE ME, SITRIC, OR I'LL COME UP THERE AND GET YA!

*Horse, harp and sword of light war-banner sold separately

Because there was so much fighting going on during this time, very few people lived a long life in Ireland. Maybe that's where the legend of *Tír na nÓg* (The Land of Youth) came from – hardly anyone lived long enough to grow old! But BB managed to. He was in his 70s or 80s when the Battle of Clontarf was fought. His sons led the fighting while he prayed in his tent. So his action figure might've more realistically looked like this:

BRIAN BORU INACTION FIGURE

*Accessories include walking stick, ear-trumpet, walking frame and wee gold cross

SAYS 4 PHRASES:

1. EH? SPEAK UP!

2. NO NEED TO SHOUT!

3. GET OUT OF MY GARDEN, YOU DIRTY, STINKIN' KIDS!

4. BRODIR! WHAT ARE YOU DOING IN MY TENT WITH THAT AXE?!

*Nurse and tent sold separately

Brian became King of Munster after his older brother Mahon was murdered by a rival king. Once he'd taken revenge, he ruthlessly fought with Vikings and other clans in Munster, gaining more power and influence. Just like levelling-up in a video game, he couldn't stop! He had to go on! He wanted it all! He wanted to be ...
King of Ireland!

Brian was very clever in his quest to become Top Dog. He married his sons and daughters off to rival royal clans, to 'keep it in the family' and so strengthen his power. He also ruthlessly stamped out any resistance to his rule, imposing harsh tributes — a fancy word for protection money — on his subjects.

That's how he got the name Boru (his real name was Brian Mac Cennétig) which means 'tributes'. But because he had been so ruthless on his climb to the top, he made many enemies and they weren't just Vikings. In fact, at this point the Vikings had been living among the Irish for about 180 years. They could no longer be considered wholly Viking any more. They were part Viking, part Irish. What historians call Hiberno-Norse.

They say keep your friends close and your enemies closer. But many of Brian's enemies were members of his own family – you can't get much closer than that! Viking warriors fought on both sides of the battle, so don't believe what you hear about BB kicking the Vikings out of Ireland* or that the Vikings wanted to invade Ireland and Brian stopped them. It was more like a big family feud. It's a bit convoluted, so here's more merchandise to help explain it – a Battle of Clontarf commemorative sticker album! Collect 'em all!

*If the Vikings had been 'kicked out' in 1014, why was there a longship found in Denmark made from trees felled in Glendalough, Co. Wicklow in 1042?

BRIAN BORU who's who

King of Ireland

BB's son

UNDER THE 'SWORD OF LIGHT' BANNER

BB's 15-year-old grandson

Former King of Ireland, Máel formed an uneasy alliance with BB and shared Ireland for a while.

BB's brother. Sounds suspiciously like a Viking name. Some have identified Wolf as a brother of Brian's named Cuiduligh, but we can't be sure.

BB allied with various Irish tribes, mostly from Munster, as well as troops from Alba (Scotland), Norwegian Vikings and some pagan Manx Vikings.

UNDER THE 'RAVEN' BANNER

SITRIC SILKBEARD

Hiberno-Norse King of Dublin. BB's son-in-law AND stepson (BB was once married to Sitric's mother, Gormflaith).

SLÁINE

Sitric's wife and BB's daughter. He married her off to Sitric after Sitric staged a failed rebellion against BB in AD999 (the Battle of Glen Máma). She may be married to Sitric but her loyalties lie with BB.

MÁEL MÓRDA

King of Leinster. Gormflaith's brother. Sitric's uncle. He was once dragged out of his hiding place in a yew tree by Murchad, Brian's son, after the Battle of Glen Máma. Though he only properly fell out with Murchad over a chess game! Kind of BB's arch nemesis.

GORMFLAITH

Sitric's mother. Irish noblewoman. BB's third wife. Cunning and sneaky. She promised two different Viking earls – Sigurd and Brodir – she would marry them if they killed BB!

SIGURD

Earl of Orkney. One of the earls Gormflaith promised to marry if he killed BB.

BRODIR

Earl of Man. The other earl Gormflaith promised to marry. Sigurd and Brodir would also have been attracted to Gormflaith's wealth and status.

The Battle OF Clontarf STICKER COLLECTION

SPOILER ALERT! By the time the battle is over in the evening of 23 April 1014* all but five of these people will be DEAD!

But *which* five? If you already know, don't be telling anybody just yet. The Battle of Clontarf was the closest thing to the All-Ireland you could get back then, so let our two commentators, Brother Conor and Brother Liam tell you all about it.** Because it's so gruesome we're not actually allowed to show you any of the battle itself, but you'll get the drift.

*Some people think this date, which was Good Friday, was made up to make Brian look even holier. Others say the battle wasn't even fought at Clontarf!

**It was Irish monks who wrote down the story of the battle many years later at the request of BB's great grandson. Needless to say, they were a bit biased!

132

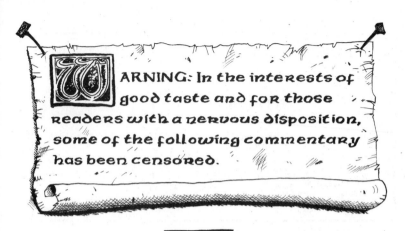

Er, thanks, lads — you were very helpful. Yes, the battle was pretty gory. Thousands of men on both sides were killed or maimed. Vikings drowned trying to get to their ships, weighed down by their heavy armour. Many more were cut down at a bridge while retreating to the safety of Dublin. Only twenty made it back to the city alive!

And what happened to Brian? Some retreating Vikings led by Brodir, the Viking earl from the Isle of Man, spotted Brian's tent, snuck in and cut off Brian's head while he prayed. A different story says that Brian hacked off Brodir's legs at the same time as Brodir embedded an axe in Brian's brain. A good story, but likely untrue because yet *another* story says that Brian's brother, Wolf the Quarrelsome, hunted down Brodir and finished him off.

Brian Boru's army may have won the battle but BB lost not only his own life, but those of his sons and heirs, his grandson and many soldiers, friends and family. So many that it was next to impossible to crown anyone king in his place. So Máel Sechnaill, who was King before Brian and who is thought not to have fought at Clontarf, became King of Ireland again. He said this about the battle:

> I NEVER SAW A BATTLE LIKE IT, NOR HAVE I HEARD OF ITS EQUAL; AND EVEN IF AN ANGEL OF GOD ATTEMPTED ITS DESCRIPTION, I DOUBT IF HE COULD GIVE IT.

King Sitric Silkbeard, who had watched the whole battle with his mother Gormflaith from the safety of his fortress, stayed on as king of Dublin. Gormflaith didn't have to marry either Sigurd or Brodir as they were both killed. Sláine (who was BB's daughter, remember) is said to have taunted her husband Sitric about BB's victory:

> IT APPEARS TO ME THAT THE FOREIGNERS HAVE GAINED THEIR INHERITANCE.

In other words, Sitric's defeat was well deserved.

Brian's bones are now buried in a wall of St. Patrick's Cathedral in Armagh.

Here's a useful map showing the whole battle.

You're welcome!

NORSE SENSE

VIKING LEGACY

A legacy is something that people leave behind after they're dead and gone, something for future generations to remember them by. Brian Boru became a symbol for hope and the unification of Ireland, even if

CONAN O'BRIEN,
AMERICAN
ENTERTAINER

MICHAEL O'BRIEN,
IRISH PUBLISHER

DARA O'BRIAIN,
IRISH COMEDIAN

in reality he could be quite merciless! BB left plenty of descendants behind to carry on his legacy — one of the most common names in Ireland is O'Brien and there are loads of famous actors, politicians, sportspeople, artists *(and publishers!)* with the surname.

The Vikings left a lasting legacy too. There are very few people who wouldn't recognise a Viking warrior like this, even though they never had horns on their helmets!

The world over remembers Viking culture in ways they may not even realise. For instance, some of the days of the week are named after their gods, such as Wednesday (Woden's day): after Odin, who was also known as Woden. Thursday (Thor's day): after the thunder god Thor. Friday (Frigga's day): after Frigga, the goddess of marriage

Vikings appear in films, TV shows, video games, comics, cartoons and books. Practically every fantasy film set in the distant past has a Viking flavour to the costumes and sets. We just can't get enough!

Even modern technology has a Viking influence – Bluetooth is named after the famous Viking, Harald Bluetooth and the Bluetooth symbol is made from the Viking runes for Harald's initials, H.B. Why was he nicknamed Bluetooth?

Some people think it's because he had a bad tooth that looked darker than the rest of his teeth. But there is evidence that some Vikings coloured their teeth as a fashion!

There are dozens of modern-day words in English that have a Viking origin. Which of these are Viking words? **Answers below.**

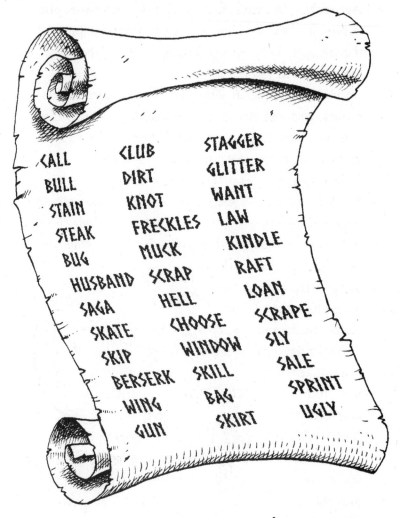

CALL
CLUB
STAGGER
BULL
DIRT
GLITTER
STAIN
KNOT
WANT
STEAK
FRECKLES
LAW
BUG
MUCK
KINDLE
HUSBAND
SCRAP
RAFT
SAGA
HELL
LOAN
SKATE
CHOOSE
SCRAPE
SKIP
WINDOW
SLY
BERSERK
SKILL
SALE
WING
BAG
SPRINT
GUN
SKIRT
UGLY

ANSWER: All of them!

Vikings have left a lasting legacy on Irish culture too. There were no towns and cities in Ireland before the Norsemen arrived, and places like Dublin, Limerick and Waterford quickly became major trade centres for visitors from all over Europe. Vikings may have pillaged monasteries in the early days but the truth is they really were no worse than the Irish who happily slaughtered monks and stole their riches much more often than the Vikings did!

We have no stuff left to steal!

Most Vikings were peaceful farmers, traders and settlers more than they were marauding, murdering maniacs. In a pretty short space of time they settled down amongst the Irish and the two cultures mingled. Their houses, clothes, jewellery and art were a mixture of two styles. From what was found in the Wood Quay excavations, we can easily see that the people of Viking-age Dublin were very civilized. The Vikings never 'invaded' Ireland any more than Brian Boru 'kicked them out'. So next time someone says that the Vikings were just murdering invaders, you can tell them that they were just really **DEADLY!**

TIMELINE

795 – The first recorded Viking attacks occur on monasteries on Rechru Island, Inishmurray and Inishbofin.

798–807 – Having figured out monasteries were full of unprotected gold – and Vikings love their bling – Viking raids start happening more often.

811–12 – The Irish strike back when the warriors of Ulaid in the north-east defeat a band of Viking raiders. Then the men of Umall, Co. Mayo and the King of Eóganacht Locha Léin in the south-west slaughter a load of Vikings.

824 – Vikings raid Skellig Michael off the south-west coast and capture the abbot called Étgal for a ransom. When nobody pays up, they starve him to death.

825 – Again, the Ulaid defeat the Vikings.

835 – The Irish defeat Vikings at Derry.

836 – Starting to get cheeky now, the first inland (not on the coast) raid by the Vikings takes place on the lands of the southern Uí Néill (Co. Meath), where they kill loads of people and take lots of captives. Also, they raid Connacht in the west.

837 – Having decided they rather like Ireland, hordes of Vikings arrive in sixty ships and this time they go further inland up the Rivers Liffey and Boyne. They plunder farms, churches and fortresses.

840–41 – Vikings spend the whole winter on Lough Neagh.

841–42 – Vikings start building fortified bases called *longphuirt* around the country and stay the winter in Dublin. The first Irish-Viking alliance is formed.

845 – The High King of Ireland captures and drowns a Viking leader called Thorgest. The Vikings capture the abbot of Armagh called Forannán but he returns home the following year.

848–9 – Utterly sick of their carry-on, the Irish start winning loads of battles against the Vikings.

851–852 – Danish Vikings arrive and attack the Norwegian Vikings, wanting to take control of Dublin. They fight a massive sea battle in Carlingford Lough.

902 – Irish clans seize Dublin. Vikings flee to Britain.

917 – Vikings return to Dublin and take it back.

928 – Viking massacre at Dunmore Cave, Kilkenny.

936 – Irish burn Dublin down but the Vikings quickly build it up again.

976–978 – Brian Boru becomes king of the Dal gCais, defeats Vikings and takes Limerick. Then becomes King of Munster.

980 – High King Máel Sechnaill seizes Dublin then the Vikings take it back.

997 – Brian and Máel agree to divide Ireland equally between them – Brian as King of the South (except Dublin), and Máel as King of the North.

999–1001 – Brian breaks the agreement. Abandoned by his allies, Máel submits to Brian.

1001–1013 – Brian expands his territories and becomes King of Ireland (except Dublin) in 1002. Ireland is quite peaceful for a while. But Brian has stepped on lots of toes on his way to the top and his enemies wait for a chance to take him down, especially Máel Morda, King of Leinster. (Is *everyone* called Máel?!)

1014 – Nothing of interest happens this year. Oh wait! Just the Battle of Clontarf in April! BB and Máel Morda are killed and Máel Sechnaill takes over as High King. Viking power in Ireland is greatly reduced.

1014–1042 – Sitric Silkbeard stays on as King of Dublin until 1036. He dies in exile four years later. The Vikings integrate completely with the Irish, becoming Christians and generally behaving themselves.

1169 – The Norman Invasion of Ireland (not an invasion by people called Norman, no) begins, but that's another story ...

1) Weaving loom. wool comes from the family's sheep. Clothes, blankets, tapestries and even ships' sails are made on the loom.

2) An iron (made from heated glass) for pressing clothes. The board is made from whalebone.

3) Tallow (animal fat) candles

4) Tapestries to decorate the walls and keep heat in.

5) Weapon and shield display on wall.

6) Clay jugs and jars, all imported.

7) Soupstone bowl

8) Quern-stone for grinding grain to make bread.

9) Rye or barley bread baking on skillets.

10) Iron or soapstone cooking pot.

11) Wooden bucket, bowl and plate.

12) Metal knives and spoons but no forks – they haven't been invented yet!

13) Cushions and furs.

143

ANSWERS TO FISHAMBLE STREET

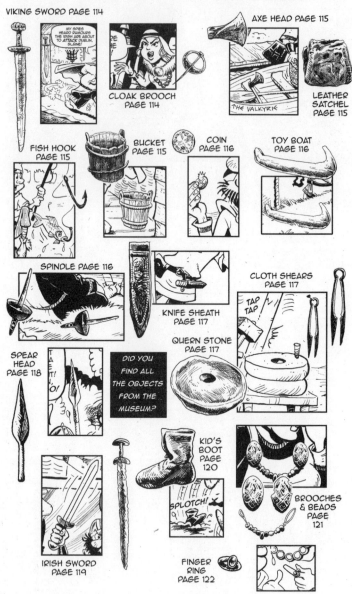

VIKING SWORD PAGE 114

MY SPIES HEARD RUMOURS THE IRISH ARE ABOUT TO ATTACK DUBLIN, SLUINE!

CLOAK BROOCH PAGE 114

AXE HEAD PAGE 115

LEATHER SATCHEL PAGE 115

FISH HOOK PAGE 115

BUCKET PAGE 115

COIN PAGE 116

TOY BOAT PAGE 116

THE VALKYRIE

SPINDLE PAGE 116

KNIFE SHEATH PAGE 117

CLOTH SHEARS PAGE 117

TAP TAP

QUERN STONE PAGE 117

SPEAR HEAD PAGE 118

DID YOU FIND ALL THE OBJECTS FROM THE MUSEUM?

KID'S BOOT PAGE 120

SPLOTCH!

BROOCHES & BEADS PAGE 121

IRISH SWORD PAGE 119

FINGER RING PAGE 122